God is Good!

Leading Children to Jesus...

Shelley Safrit

WestBow Press books may be ordered through booksellers or by contacting:

WestBow Press
A Division of Thomas Nelson & Zondervan
1663 Liberty Drive
Bloomington, IN 47403
www.westbowpress.com
844-714-3454

Scripture quotations are from the ESV® Bible (The Holy Bible, English Standard Version®), copyright © 2001 by Crossway, a publishing ministry of Good News Publishers. Used by permission. All rights reserved.

ISBN: 978-1-6642-5262-2 (sc)
ISBN: 978-1-6642-5263-9 (e)

Library of Congress Control Number: 2021924901

Print information available on the last page.

WestBow Press rev. date: 03/07/2023

WESTBOW
PRESS®
A DIVISION OF THOMAS NELSON
& ZONDERVAN

Leading Children to Jesus...

"I have no greater joy than to hear that my
children are walking in the truth."
3 John 1:4

To: _____

From: _____

Written to all the children of the world...

Jesus loves you...

...but Jesus said, "Let the little children come to me and do not hinder them, for to such belongs the kingdom of heaven."

Matthew 19:14

It is amazing! In the beginning, God created the earth we live on. He created it in 7 days. Where is your home on the earth? What is the name of your country? Can you name the seven days of the week? Repeat after me: Monday, Tuesday, Wednesday, Thursday, Friday, Saturday, and Sunday! Now, let us see what God created on each day!

Gen 1:1

John 1:1–3

At first there was only darkness
and on day 1, God spoke,
and light appeared. He called
the light, day. He called the
dark, night. Isn't it good that
we do not have to be in the
dark all the time? God gives
us light so we can see all the
beautiful things He made!

Gen 1:3-5

On day 2, He made the sky. There were clouds above and waters below. What colors are the clouds and what are some of the colors of the waters?

Gen 1:6-8

On day 3, God gathered the waters into their own places – lakes, creeks, oceans, rivers. He created the dry ground, and all the trees and plants that grow on the earth. Are there certain places where you like to swim, fish, or boat? Name some of those places. Let us name some of the larger oceans together: Atlantic, Pacific, Indian, and Arctic. Look on a world map to see where each one is located. God's trees and flowers are beautiful. Look out the window and name some of your favorites.

Gen 1:9-13

On, day 4, God created the moon to light the night.
He created the sun to light the day. He created the stars.

Because of the moon, we have seasons. Let us name the four
seasons: spring, summer, fall, winter. Describe each one.

DAY

NIGHT

Because of the sun, the plants grow, and we have food to eat
every day. Isn't it wonderful how God provides for us!

Because of the stars, the sky is beautiful, and they are a guide
at night, especially to ships on the oceans. Did you know that
no matter where you live on the earth, you can see the stars?
Enjoy an evening looking at the night sky! God is so good!

Gen 1:14-19

On day 5, God made the fish and all the creatures that live in the waters, and all the birds that fly in the sky. What are some of God's birds that you see from your backyard? What is your favorite fish? Name other creatures that live in the sea which God made.

Gen 1:20-23

On day 6, God made all the land animals we enjoy today, and He made you and me in His image. God began by creating Adam, the man, from the dust of the earth. Then, while God caused a deep sleep to come over Adam, God took a rib from the man's side and created Eve, the woman. He blessed them and told them to have children. God provides a special plan for you while you are on the earth He created!

Gen 1:24-31

Gen 2:18-23

Name some land animals that you really like! What sounds do they make? God is so good!

9

God created the beautiful world in which we live. On day 7, God rested. All that He made was very good! What are some of your favorite things God made? I am glad God rested, aren't you? We can rest by setting a day aside to spend time with Him in prayer, worshipping Him with others, and reading our Bible, God's Holy Word.

Gen 2:1-3

After God created the world, Adam and Eve walked with God. God provided food and shelter for them. He told them not to eat from or even touch the tree of the knowledge of good and evil, for then they would die. God warned Adam and Eve because He loved them. God loves us too. He does not want us to do things that will make Him sad. He does not want us to do things that will hurt us.

Gen 2:15-17

But, then, God's enemy, the serpent, also called satan or the devil, lied to Eve by saying she would not die if she went against what God said. So, Eve believed the lie. She chose to listen to the serpent. She did not listen to God. Eve took the fruit of the tree of the knowledge of good and evil and ate it and gave it to Adam and He ate it, too. Oh, no! Adam and Eve did something wrong. They disobeyed God.

Gen 3:1-6
Gen 3:12-13

Obey God	Disobey God
God's choices	serpent/satan/devil's choices
Turn away from sin	Sin
Right	Wrong
Good	Evil

Disobeying God is called sin. People can now choose to obey God and do good or choose to disobey God and do bad. God created us! He wants us to choose to do right because we love him. Look at the things in the right column above that go against God. The things of God are in the left column. Compare the two and talk about the differences.

Joshua 24:15
Psalm 37:27
James 4:7

Doing bad things causes sin to live in our hearts. But God created our hearts to be a place for Him to live, not sin.

Romans 1:20,21
Romans 3:23

God wanted to live in our heart so much, He sent His only Son, Jesus, to die on the cross so sin would die in our hearts, and our hearts could be filled with God and His love. God is so good.

John 3:16-18
John 1:14

When we tell Jesus we are sorry for our sins, He forgives us.

When He forgives us, we are set free from sin and death. Our hearts become clean and new, and we can walk with God! We can have the free gift of God, through Jesus, which is eternal life.

Romans 6:22
2 Corinthians 5:17

Eternal life means living with Jesus forever. Jesus will live in our hearts through His Holy Spirit while we are on the earth He created. He will help us make choices that please Him and help us live the life He wants for us. We find how He wants us to live when we read His Word, the Bible. One day, we will live with Him in Heaven where He will make all things new. This is a free gift for all people who ask Him.

Romans 6:23

Will you open this free gift and ask Jesus to live in your heart?
He created you in His image and He loves you so very much.
Say this prayer and let Him live in your heart.

Romans 10:9-13

Dear God,

I choose You and want to make choices that please You. I know I can only do this when You live in me. So I ask You, Jesus, to forgive me of my sins and live in my heart through Your Holy Spirit. Jesus, thank You for dying on the cross for my sins and help me to live for You by doing things that make You happy. Thank You for Your Word, the Bible. Help me to read and to pray to You each day, and I know I will grow strong in You. Thank You for giving me eternal life so I can live with You forever in Heaven.

In Jesus' Name I ask and pray.
Amen.

John 1:12-13
Romans 8:16

Because you prayed this prayer you are now a part of God's family. You are His child. You have received His free gift of eternal life through His Son, Jesus. God is so good!

You can write your name and today's date here as a reminder that on this day you asked Jesus into your heart.

_____

Name   Date

1 John 5:13
1 John 3:1–3

This is the start of your journey with Jesus, the Son of God, who loves you more than anyone and who will be your very best friend forever!

Jeremiah 29:11
Romans 8:38–39
Hebrews 12:1–3

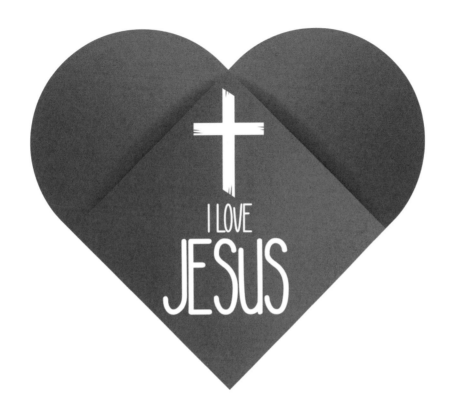

Keep this little book in a special place
as a reminder that God lives in your heart
through His Holy Spirit, Who will help you live your life for Jesus.
Galatians 2:20
Ephesians 3:17
Colossians 1:27

...not by might, nor by power, but by my Spirit,
says the Lord of hosts.
Zechariah 4:6

A Note from the Author:

. . . .

God is Good! is a book created with love to reach children of all ages. The idea was birthed from a grandmother, Leslie Overby, who desired that her grandchildren come to genuinely know the truth of God's Word and come to personally know Jesus as their Savior. Through prayer and contemplation, this book became a reality. May blessings from Jesus reside on you as you share His Word with those around you, those you love so dearly. There is no greater Father, Friend, Savior, or Provider than the Lord our God, and His love for us is deeper than we will ever be able to comprehend. "For I am sure that neither death nor life, nor angels nor rulers, nor things present nor things to come, nor powers, nor height nor depth, nor anything else in all creation, will be able to separate us from the love of God in Christ Jesus our Lord." Romans 8:38,39.

Sincerely,
Shelley Safrit

About the Author

. . . .

Shelley received Jesus into her life in 1994. Since then, her writings have come from her quiet times spent with the Lord. She enjoys writing poetry, plays, and stories. It is her prayer that the Lord would use this little book for children everywhere to know and understand how much Jesus loves them. May you find Jesus close, as you explore together the great adventure God has for all of us who love and know Him.

Other books written by Shelley Safrit:
The Path of Prayer, A Quarterly Poem Prayer Journal (2019)

Acknowledgements

. . . .

This book is a result of the loving encouragement, vision, and friendship of several people including Leslie Overby, Margaret Smith, Dee Vazquez, Sharon Leach, and Lavonne Stone. I am grateful to each one for their heartfelt love, undying truth of God's Word, and desire to minister to all children.

And for my husband, Glenn, and our two sons, Samuel and Jesse for their constant and loving support for the things of the Lord.

Printed in the United States
by Baker & Taylor Publisher Services